LIVING LIFE WITH DIABETES
THEN SOME AND MORE

RODNEY RICKS

NEWMAN SPRINGS PUBLISHING
320 Broad Street
Red Bank, NJ 07701

First originally published by Newman Springs Publishing 2024

ISBN 979-8-89308-314-9 (Paperback)
ISBN 979-8-89308-315-6 (Digital)

Printed in the United States of America

was born in 1970. My mother, Mary Ricks, and my father, Ocie Ricks, saw me growing up. As a kid, my mom, dad, me, my brother, and my sister lived in Tallassee City in Alabama, a small community with a big heart. We didn't have much, but we had each other, and that's all that mattered to me. Growing up there was alright, but I really didn't like it there. My two cousins always double-teamed me, and it was boring there too. There were parks, and recreation connections they had too, only stores one or two miles away you had to walk to if you didn't have a bike or a car to drive.

See, what I am trying to tell you is that streets down there are nothing like the streets up here. Roads go down and up like hills. On a bike? Good luck. You have to go down a hill at least fifty miles per hour or more until you come up, and better know what you are doing, or you will die for real. Roads down there, with their hills, are a lot different. They have dirt roads, red dirt, and red ants that will bite you. I was glad we moved from Tallassee City in Alabama to the big city of Detroit, Michigan. Different from the city of Tallassee, Alabama, a small community of about five thousand or so. Now life for me and my family was way better.

When we got here, Mom and Dad both got jobs working at Ford Motor Company. Mom working in the morning, Dad working midnights, we didn't want anything. Ford Motor Company had my mom and dad's back, so we found a house on the west side of the city block, Ward Street, D off, War Street, West Chicago, Joy Road.

Long story short, there were beautiful green trees all down the block, everywhere on Ward Street. Pretty houses, Detroit, Michigan. Was it in the '70s, '80s, '90s? Growing up as a kid, everything was going on in Detroit, Michigan, the motor city. But things got bad around the neighborhood years later, passing by as I was getting older. A new pair of tennis shoes going to school, you always had to watch your back. If you didn't, you'd get jacked in the '80s and '90s when going to school by gangs. Police were bad back in those days. Starter jackets, sheepskin coats, hats, boots, and nanny goat coats, jungle boots too, were something else. We used to go to Belle Isle Park, Ford Wyoming drive-in theater, State Fair Ground, Boblo Island, and many other places.

See, I want laughter, joy, and peace in my life. A quitter? No, because I keep my head to the sky. Not walking around with my head hung down to the ground. No, that's not me, because life is too short. My world, my book, my story. Seeing a mind is a terrible thing to waste. Not wasting mine, 2022 is gone, and 2023 is in the house now. New year, new life, new everything. Happy wife, happy life. I want to go to new places, see new things, go to new events, and be in a different environment without conflict in my life. Not perfect, this I know, but I'm still living, thank God.

See, I am not going to give up on life. See, I am going to be all I can be and keep hope alive as an author, amen. Writing a book is a challenge, demanding thought and knowledge—it is not a game. Tears? Yes, I cried to release the pain I feel, the pain I go through when writing this book for the world to read. Rodney Ricks, the author, is the last one left of the family.

See, I rebuke the devil in the name of Jesus, amen. I am an author. I hold a beast in me, a humble and good-hearted sinner. I have angels on my shoulder, and wings on my back, for I am an Aquarius.

A newborn baby wrapped in plastic in a duffle bag with an umbilical cord attached to it was so sad to see on TV today. I cried,

"What is the world coming to, man?" No heart, cold as the winter snow. No mind, body, no soul. Doing that to a newborn precious baby girl was cold-hearted murder, and the perpetrator would be judged down the line by God.

My brother was cooking everything in one boiling hot pot that fell on his feet. Talking about a chicken with its head cut off, he was running around the house like one, let me tell you when that hot boiling pot of whatever he was cooking fell on his feet. But anyway, he healed from that. He went to the bar with Kevin one day and got into it with some guy there. The next morning, I woke up, and my brother was cut up from head to toe, nearly dying. The boy always had some trouble hanging out with his friend Kevin at the bar. But anyway, he healed from that too.

He had driven a little blue car everywhere with everybody in it. The little blue car never let him down until the engine blew. He loved that little blue car. One day, the truck ran out of gas. I walked up to the corner. A race was going on a quarter-mile away. So the next thing I noticed, the cars took off, and one lost control and was coming at me a quarter-mile away; the lady behind me may rest in peace. She and I both got hit, and she was killed. Another guy out there got hit by the U-Haul place next door. And all the trucks were there at the time. One big propane tank was inside the U-Haul place at the time too. If it weren't for the yellow poles that weren't out there at the time he hit us, he would have run into the big propane tank and would have killed us all. Why were the police out there watching the race go on, not stopping anything? I had a lawsuit against them, but I lost it. Man, I was mad. But life goes on. My book, my story, my life. All the people take part in this story too.

There was a little small deli we had on the corner of Ward Street. Fred used to run it. He made the best cinnamon rolls in the city on our side of the block, the big ones. He always locked the gate to the store, but for some reason, somebody always got in the gate and stole the whole tray of donuts. And when Fred came back and saw the gate unlocked, the whole tray of donuts was gone. Man, he was mad and upset, but those were the days when Fred was up there. Then the old man Omar had it. It was his home with all the dogs he loved. Then it became a police station, a beauty salon, I mean some of everything.

I hate that my cousin fell asleep going to work. A truck crushed him while sleeping. He should have stayed home that day, but he didn't. May he rest in peace. Up on the back porch, guess what happens next? The whole porch fell down. Guess who fell with it? Yes, my cousin. Thought he was dead, but he wasn't. Thank God. We were at his house, up in the attic. No, we shouldn't be up there, right? Guess what happened next. He fell through the ceiling, putting a big hole in it. I left, knowing Uncle John was going to kill him once he saw the ceiling.

But anyway, I was riding with my uncle Don one night in his brand-new car. A big rat came running across the dashboard, and we stopped, jumping out of the car at the red light. Sitting on the porch at my aunt's house, right, enjoying the music and barbecue, laughing, joking, another big rat from out of nowhere came from out of the bushes onto the first step of the porch. So my uncle called himself stomping at the rat.

Long story short, the rat stood up on its two back legs through his pals. Everybody ran. Boy, let me tell you, I don't know what's up with me and those rats. Over at my girlfriend's house, my friend and I went to the store, got something to drink, and came back with a half-gallon of gin and ten beers. Just the two of us drinking, we drank everything we got from the store. I was driving my mother's brand-new car. Long story short, I forgot I had the hot burning grill in the back seat of the car, and the next thing I noticed, the police were behind us. I was so drunk, trying to keep my composure, but I couldn't. But anyway, they got out of the car, the grill smoking hot in the back seat of the car, just burning a big hole in the seat of the car. So they told him to drive. He was drunk too, but they still let him drive, for some reason. Maybe because they knew I was drunker than him. They knew my mother was going to kill me when I got home. By the grace of God, we made it to my mother's house and pulled up in the driveway, back seat smoking. My brother came out and ran back into the house, telling Mom. She came out with the broomstick, and I got beat down with it. So now I was mad, walking up to the corner of Ward Street, lying in the middle of the street, drunk and dumb. Glad nothing was coming down the street at the time. Nelson came and got me out of the street. Never will I drink ten beers and a half-gallon of gin again. That's why I don't drink that much today. My body can't take it anymore.

Just saw on TV an eleven-month-old baby in Tampa in a van, carjacked inside, found safe, and not harmed. Thank God. This is the world we live in. We can't even go to the gas station without people getting shot, mentally ill, or messed up in the head. A boy killed a cop on Joy Road. Sad, may he rest in peace. There are tragedies all around the world. But what can you do but live? And my life, living it with diabetes, the first time having it sucks because it is a deadly disease, a natural-born killer disease in the world too. Scientists need to come up with a cure soon, and I mean very soon, like tomorrow, because diabetes is just killing people every day. The world you and I live in too. And the thing about diabetes is it involves monitoring your sugar, making sure that it doesn't go too high or too low. Not a good feeling, let me tell you, not a good feeling at all when it drops on you. Talking about being jittery and having anxiety and feeling scared too when it drops—it can be alarming, especially when it is out of control, and you know it to be very scary. Let me tell you, it's the number one natural-born killer, a disease you don't want to have either.

And man, the dream I have in my head, always had, for life, to build my own house out of my initials, R. R., for the world, my world, to see and come to from all around the world. Can you imagine? Do you know how many people from around the world would come just to see my house, so amazed by it too because never ever have they seen a house, the first house to make out his own initial for the world to see but me, genius. See, everyone else who's rich in this world takes their money and does what with it, I don't know, don't care either. Like Scarface said, I want everything to come to me, everything in it, to the world. I mean, think about it, my house would be all over the TV, world news, local news, all news everywhere, from around the world to all because of the house that rock built out of his initial, the first one ever in the world to come up with an idea to build a house out of his initial, the first one ever, too genius. Why has everybody else buying houses or building them never thought about this one before? Never, no one but me.

See, my mind is so creative and filled with so much knowledge that God has gifted me with; I have to say, "Thank you, Lord, for all you have done for me and are still doing for me." Why am I here on this earth? I know that all this is just temporary too. But anyway, just sitting here thinking about the people who are homeless, outside in the cold, and with nowhere to go, is very sad to me. The money all these rich people have in the world, with a heart, or who have a heart, could feed a lot of people in the world, but they don't choose to do that because they find other things to do with their money besides helping people who are in need, struggling in the world. It doesn't need to be that way. Why and what for? But I've always said it too. If I were ever to get rich or be rich one day in my life, I would take care to feed all the homeless people I could or can feed in the world, believe that, from the heart. Nobody in the world could stop me but the Lord God above me himself. I love all my homeless people outside in the streets, struggling to keep warm out there. I pray for them every day. I see them all out there every day, too sad. But what can you do? Nothing, and truth be told, sorry to say, but half of them, if not all of them, do it to themselves too.

But what do I do? I myself am not perfect either. I am just an author trying to get by in life and live it happily. That's all I want in life—to be happy. The legacy I have to leave behind for my family is all I have. Like I said before, it's hard out here in this world with inflation rising every day, prices going up on everything sucks. Living paycheck to paycheck to live in this world today, just getting by because of a mortgage or rent bill you are behind on because inflation is so damn high now. But who am I? Like I said, I am not perfect either, at all, just me, an author for life.

Well, I could keep going on, telling you all about my world, my life, my books, too, but I'm tired. I can't think anymore; my brain said, "No more. That's all you have to give out. That's all you have left too." So why keep going, knowing that this is it? Done did it; it's a hit, a five-star book rated number one right here. The second book done by me, too, and the last one, too. If the review board doesn't like it this time, it's over for real. Tired. Sorry. I really tried hard this time to make it better than before, better than the first book I wrote, the first one ever made by me, too, and the last one left in the family too.

Depression is a deadly disease, just as bad as diabetes for people who don't know this. It is a killer. The only thing with diabetes is you have to use insulin, take a shot every day of your life, and make sure that all meds are taken to stay alive each day of your life. Depression makes you sad—when you want to give up on life and give up on faith because something inside you hurts so bad you don't want to talk about it to anybody. Depression with diabetes is a mess, like I said, two deadly diseases you don't want to play with. Living life in my world with diabetes, depression, and a mind that plays tricks on you every day of your life is not a good thing at all. Depression makes you want revenge on those who did wrong to you.

Depression compels you to take actions you wouldn't normally consider when things aren't going your way. Between depression and diabetes, there's no winning; both are deadly, naturally born killer diseases that kill everyone, every day—this is a serious matter. The feeling of depression, coupled with diabetes and a broken heart, is overwhelming, especially because of how it affects you when you've never had it before but are now diagnosed at the age of fifty. This has led to significant life changes for me. It necessitated a change in my lifestyle; I realized I had to change if I wanted to continue living in my world and enjoy my life.

The experience of living with depression and diabetes in a world filled with evil, diseases, and naturally deadly killers is disheartening for everyone who lives in it. We are all waiting for scientists to come up with a cure for all diseases, and it would be extraordinary if they found one for depression. But, as we know, that's the life we live, having both depression and diabetes at the same time doesn't mix well.

This book, written by me, Rodney Ricks, shares my world, life, and experience with depression and diabetes. I am the last Ricks in the family, the only man left besides my father. It's bewildering to witness diseases spreading across the world, with no one knowing where they come from and no cures available until much later, after hundreds of thousands of people have died. Why is that? Man-made diseases are killing everyone, slowly, and we are all too aware of it.

Technology is improving each day, but it's not coming up with a cure fast enough for all of us living in this world that's filled with all kinds of diseases—deadly, man-made, natural-born, and killers too. It's funny how we just got over COVID-19 after two long years of staying in the house, really not going anywhere unless we had to. Now, China has a new disease, another one we all don't know anything about that's a killer, and we don't even know it yet—crazy. Our world and lives are marred with diseases, man-made, just killing us slowly. When is it all going to end? Stop. Let us live. Let us all die of old age like God wants us to go, to be. He surely didn't want us going out like that because of man-made diseases, let me tell you that, but who am I? Just me, one person, one man too, telling the truth about what's going on here today in our world. You have to be strong today, every day, in this time, life, present, future, and place we live in, or you die—just keeping it real.

Navigating life with diabetes in a world filled with diseases, deadly, natural-born, and killers too is an ongoing challenge. This book encapsulates my world and my feelings too, offering insights about me, about life, about a world we all live in, just filled with diseases—deadly forces in this world. We are all on Earth just temporarily, I hope you all know that too, so you better live life as happily as you can and not be sad because living for today—here today, gone tomorrow, hear me. It's not living here today, gone tomorrow anymore. Now it's living here today, gone today, and tomorrow. Why is that?

I had to change it up again, and for the very last time too because if it doesn't make it this time, at least I can say one thing as a strong Black man God made me out to be. I wasn't a quitter; I put all I had into it and some too. It was a challenge, brain thinking as well too. All my people are in it, even if I didn't say your names, you're in it, bet that too. Too many names, and too many people I know. Feel me? It's better this way too, to tell you all I didn't forget anybody.

Don't need anybody saying he didn't put me in his second book just like the first one he wrote and had published too.

The first book, "God Will Tell You That, Boy," really came to me in an unexpected way. I don't know how it happened; I was just sitting up in my room, picked up a pen, and started writing. My musings were about life and the block I live on—Ward Street, Block D, off War Street. Those were the days, up the stairs in that room where I lived. I sure do miss that, but now I'm older, and life goes on for me. Just being here, I've put a lot of work into this book to make it right for the board this time. I hope and pray for its success. There's a long way to go, but a short time to get there, and I am committed to doing whatever it takes by all means necessary.

Because I am me—a Black, strong man, and the author of this book, the last one left in the family, but still going because God wills it, boy. I thank God every day, first thing in the morning when I wake up and when I go to sleep. Amen. All I can say is, if it wasn't for him, there would be no me. In Jesus's name, I pray, amen. Here some, there some, every day, when I feel like writing about my life, my world, my story, my feelings too.

The truth be told to you and all, see, my book here isn't just about my world; it's about living life with diabetes, my story being told to the world. Real life, real struggle. Note and quote that this is a never-ending disease for me, for you, and for all in the world who have it, until they come up with a cure for this most deadly disease we face. Damn if you do and damn if you don't, try day by day, every day, to live right in this world.

Listen, whatever you read in this book I've just written, understand that not everything is the same. Some things are different this time around. I'm talking about the world you and I live in, about life, and living it with diabetes. I'm sharing my story and feelings with everyone. This new book is a mixture of all these elements.

Mom always told me to make it better if I can and that practice makes perfect. Never give up, keep on fighting until your very last breath, and hold on to your faith because that's all you've got in life, and your sanity, if you still have it. Live humbly, and live freely. Life is not promised today or tomorrow, so just live it the best you can and praise God too. We all have different feelings about different things in life, just like I said before about my feelings.

One day, perhaps, I will have that big old house, made uniquely with my initial—the first ever created by me. It would be a serious achievement, I tell you. All I need is a miracle, something swift and sudden like winning the Powerball, Mega Millions, or getting that Lucky for Life number. Then I could direct my own movies inside my own house, bypassing the entire movie industry except for myself, my family, and me. This book holds a lot, and people don't even know it yet, not until they read this particular edition. It's a six-star compilation of feelings, stories, life experiences, and living with diabetes, with a bit extra thrown in. As an entrepreneur striving in many ventures, I'm willing to do whatever it takes. My dad always said you have to start somewhere, even if it's from the bottom.

To write a book, one needs six senses and a brilliant mind and brain. It's my choice to decide which to use when making decisions. So choose wisely, hear me out—real talk. My book, about a world of diabetes life filled with feelings, is written by yours truly, Rodney Ricks, the last one left in my family. All this is written down and ready to be shared again for all to read upon publication. This is the final story by Mr. Ricks, truly known as Money Rich, the last author and diabetes man you see here. There's no one more like me, except for my son, whom I've brought into this world and life.

Every day is a different struggle; my sugar levels are out of control. I'm sick and tired of this relentless battle. When will it end? Oh Lord, scientists need to hurry up and find a cure for diabetes. Living with this every day is a hardship for everyone afflicted. You know exactly what I'm talking about. I cry my eyes out because I want it to end. This feeling breaks you down to your knees, making you question why it had to be you who was burdened with such a terrible and deadly disease. It hurts so badly that you just want to give up on everything.

It's hard to explain, and I doubt I'll ever figure it out. This constant struggle is something I never asked for in my life, yet here it is. How and from where it came, I'll probably never know.

Living with diabetes, a natural-born killer and one of the deadliest diseases in the world, truly sucks. I have a million things to say, to get off my mind and out of my soul, about this deadly disease that feels like it could kill me right now. Damn, it is what it is, but what can you do but pray and wish it away? It's something that's killing everybody, everyone too, I tell you that. Life goes on, even though living with diabetes is hard.

I don't understand why Hollywood doesn't have a spot on the ground, a star for diabetes, the number one killer in the world too. I don't know which way to go—up, down, front, back, side to side, in and out—it all sucks.

Yesterday, my friend and I were sitting in my car. Afterward, we both got out at the same time. And next thing I knew, when we got out of the car, my friend dropped and fell to the ground. It was so sudden and scared me because that had never happened to him before. I rushed around the car, and seeing him on the ground, he fell quite hard, so I asked him if he was alright. He looked up at me and said, "Yeah, right."

I said, "No, really."

He told me to wait a minute while he was still lying there on the ground. I waited for a second, then finally got him off the ground and asked him again if he was alright. He said, "Yeah, I need something to eat," and finally told the truth, which I didn't even know— all this time the boy was borderline diabetic and never told me about it until now.

So we went into my dad's house, and I sat him down because he was talking about his sugar being low. I found it a bit funny, so I went into the kitchen, and got him some sugar water, and a can of Vienna sausages with some crackers for him to eat quickly. He sat there, and I told him to drink the sugar water and eat the Vienna sausage and crackers I gave him because he started looking really bad, his sugar getting very low—a situation I had never encountered but now knew for the first time. He finally started drinking the sugar water and eating the Vienna sausage and crackers. I sat down for a minute and watched him to make sure he was alright. When we were outside, before entering the house, he fell quite hard on the ground before I got him up, so I had to keep an eye on him.

The last thing I told him before I left and walked out the door was to make sure he went to the doctor first thing in the morning because, as hard as he hit the ground, he might have a concussion and hadn't even noticed it. But I told him the rest was up to him if he wanted to live. This is just my world, my feelings, living life with diabetes, and then some.

See, this book isn't just about my life, world, feelings, and living with diabetes. My book is about everything, so you all know because trust me, nothing is the same, really, this time here in this book of mine that I wrote.

Every day, I write in my book but never know what I'm going to write until I start. Then once I get into it, I don't want to stop because I'm so engrossed. Like I said, this time you never know what's in this book I wrote until you all read this one. This time, I've switched things up, making things right for all to enjoy reading—whether it makes you laugh, cry, or both. When I start writing in my book, it's like getting behind the wheel of a brand-new car or truck and just moving forward. I'm like the little bunny on TV that keeps going and going. I'm not playing around; something has to give for me this time, which I really hope and pray for. So, I've put it all in the Lord's hands, thought about him first, and then kept it moving for real.

This book is about life, feelings, diabetes, the world, and something different in it to boost my book sales. It might get approved this time by the board—who knows? It's all in their hands now to read again and see if it's approvable. Fingers crossed, that's all I can say. See, I'm one of those who'll never quit, raised by a mother who gave birth to me with the help of the Lord above, then by my father on Earth. Like I said, you never know what I'm going to say until you read this book for yourself.

I'm telling you, I've switched everything up and made it better this time. This book is for everyone to read about life and living with diabetes—a natural, deadly killer in our world. Watching TV today, I saw they have a cure for sickle cell but not for diabetes, which is just as deadly, if not more. It makes me think there may never be a cure for diabetes.

It's a long way to go but a short time to get there, just like writing this book for everyone to read, laugh, cry, and enjoy. It is what it is, and that's all there is to it. Like it or not, nobody's a robot; that's all mine, let me tell you.

You see why people do a lot of messed-up things when depression hits them when things really are not going the way they planned or wanted—it sucks. Anger builds up so quickly inside you; you don't want to think, you just want to do something crazy all because the devil is trying to steal my joy, my heart, my mind, my soul. But I rebuke the devil in the name of Jesus, my Lord. Yes, my world, my feelings, living life with diabetes, then some depression, and everything else in life, too.

This book contains everything: my life, world, feelings, and all the things I did while writing it. I'm talking about the people I love, the good times we had growing up as kids—everything is in this book of mine. It's not just about living with diabetes; it's about feelings, and the world too. It's about how I really feel inside, what my mind, heart, and soul say—just how I feel.

Whatever comes to mind is what I pour into this book, making it a repository of thoughts. This time, it's the grand finale, the last book from me. I have to make it big and ensure this one lasts forever. It's all about securing a legacy for life, for me, and for you too. We live in a tough world, which is why I shed real tears when feeling blue. The devil tries to steal my joy, but he cannot because I hold the Lord God dear to my heart. In Jesus's name, I pray, amen. This is all about my feelings in life, the world, and my heart.

This last and final grand finale book was written by yours truly, me, Rodney Ricks. I take life one day at a time because I have to fight every day—battling feelings of depression and waking up with a disease, hoping, praying, and wondering if there will ever be a cure like those already invented by man. This makes me wonder. As I've said before and I'll say it again, this book isn't just about living life with diabetes. It encompasses much more: mind, body, and soul. No one is tired of wanting this feeling to end, yearning for a happy feeling and a cure, here and now, for real.

My book is filled with everything, everything I've put into it, all from the heart, mind, body, and soul. Watch out for this one; it's going to be big. A mind is a terrible thing to waste, and I'm not wasting mine on anyone but the Lord, God, himself. Everything I've written, and typed, all comes from me, yours truly, the last man in the family, an author, a legendary, beloved son—one any mother, father, sister, or brother could have. Life is a blessing, and that's why I thank the Lord, God, above me.

Reflecting on how I feel about everything, and then some, each day begins with gratitude as I wake up when God wakes me up first thing in the morning. But how I feel is real and true too. Better days are coming, and I'm a true believer in that.

Life is what you make of it, how you choose to live it, how you choose to love it—really. If I had the money, I would buy a cure for diabetes, one of the world's deadliest and most dangerous diseases. I hope the world, which I love so much, and the people in it, never forget this book that the last of the Ricks family wrote for all to love, laugh, and cherish joy in mind, heart, body, and soul. Feel me on this one. Everything in this book of mind, you won't understand until you read it and grasp where I'm coming from.

Writing a book and trying to convey what I'm talking about, when it comes to using the mind and brain, is not easy. It's just the way of the world when trying to write a book you love so much. Being me, as the author and the last son in my family, true to the game of book writing, involving real heart, soul, and mind, is so hard. You have to dream big if you want to achieve something or be somebody in life, in the world too. Time waits for no one, a fact not everyone realizes; life is too short, so stop playing with your life and the world.

Just trying to get by is hard. Living with diabetes sucks. It's a trip, sitting up here now, every damn minute, second, checking my diabetes to make sure it's right in the middle and not down, with that funny feeling we all know what I'm talking about—that real, funny feeling. We live in a crazy world, let me tell you. I just need to hit something like a lottery number so I can sit back, chill, live life happy with joy, and everything else, etc. I've always wanted to know how it feels to be rich, not having to care about anything else in life but waking up every day thanking the Lord first, and then carrying on with your day—rich, beautiful. I bet it's wonderful, and I want to see it for myself one day too.

All I can say is, one day when that day comes, I will be blessed like that. I will never forget where I came from either.

This one is already rated five stars, and it doesn't even have a rating yet. I'm going all out on this one, for myself, the world, life, and everything included. Let nothing hold you back in life if you can help it. So many thoughts in my head that I'm sharing with the world about life, living with diabetes, and having feelings in my heart, mind, and soul—no one could ever understand where I came from until they read the book I wrote, written by me. I bet they'll feel me on this one, yours truly, the greatest author ever to exist in the world, with feelings, etc. Like Tupac said, "Picture me rollin' all the way to the top on this one." Love you, Tupac. Dream big, dream true, for one day it will happen to you—just believe.

This grand finale, a prize-winning book, was made entirely by me, the believer of the book written by me as a blessing. I am one author who never gave up, quit, or stopped living life, which is hard, not easy, but time heals all wounds in a world we all live in too. Who's better than me to write this book for all to read? Nobody. Everything and more is in this one, I tell you. You'll like it, love it, enjoy it, or don't—all I can say is, if it's not for you, don't buy it. No harm done to me, just keeping it real.

I'm trying to be the best at what I do and what I write about— that's true, real, and about life, world feelings, and living life with diabetes, which also sucks badly. Life for me goes one day at a time, as it all can and does. I'm telling you, writing a book sucks the life right out of you. It really does. All the thinking you have to do, in a place with no one, nobody around, just peace all by yourself, helps out a lot and then some too.

Writing a book requires peace if you want it to be good and enjoyable for everyone. Minds matter, as do heart, body, and soul.

There's so much to say in such a short time while trying to write this book of mine—it's hard, not easy, let me tell you that. "Keep it moving," my mom and dad say. Never give up on the dream you wish to come true. Just believe in it, and it will happen—I bet on that too.

It is what it is, as I've said. If you like it, great; if you don't, you don't have to buy it. No harm done; just keep it moving, please. No hater here, just a real one. That's why they call me real because I'm the last and final real author there will ever be in life—that's me again. I write what I feel because I feel what I write, as an author of this world, in this time and place, here on Earth today. My mom always told me never to give up on my dream in life. If it's something you really want, go out there and get it. Never be afraid of one life, one you, one world too.

I love my girl, Jess, so much too. She's always by my side, through thick or thin, no matter what, loving unconditionally. She'd do anything for me if asked or needed, let me tell you. She's a very good girl in my life, eighteen years now and counting. Can't leave that out—she would kill me. One thing I can say is she has my back, and I have hers, no matter what. That's how we get down with one another. She is the best thing in my life, besides family, God, and my friends, I will never forget her, ever.

I'm telling you, everything and anything might be in this book I wrote, written for all in the world to read, laugh, cry, and enjoy too. Feeling me? It's a good feeling in my heart. This one is a hit because I believe in it. I wrote it. My dad always said to make it better if you can, and I'm going to make it better too. All it takes is keeping it real and believing in myself. People don't know how many times I've done this, and it was very hard, not easy either. Just to let you all know, as an author of this world today, try it. I did, done, and have already.

Ha, I never know what to say, but like I said, what's in this book I wrote, written for all to read today, read it. I had to make it better than the first book I wrote about my block on Ward Street, D off War Street. I didn't know what I was doing when writing that first book. There was something about that pencil I picked up in my hand that day; it just made me start writing, and to this day, I don't know why I did it. I guess it was God and the spirit inside me that did it. Amen.

Like I said, whatever I feel is what I say, and whatever I say is what I feel, too real. You know, being unbalanced and having neuropathy at the same time doesn't mix. Doing the one, two-step back and forth, side to side, sucks too. Hurry up, scientists. Come up with a cure for this deadly disease that's never-ending. It's funny, never-ending diseases like all the bad diseases we have here now on this Earth without a cure, that's never-ending too, sad.

We're all just temporarily here on Earth. We don't even know it. We will be gone, but all diseases in the world will still be here long after we are no more, bet you that. I don't know what's in the afterlife when we are gone, but one thing I do know: living today's life is a challenge, and hard. Faith is all I have in my life, being me, an author of this world.

Thank God, many times, for saving me and turning my life around three hundred sixty degrees. Books here have saved me, instilling faith to never quit, to never give up. They've taught me to always focus on the strength I have in mind, body, and soul, and to keep moving as long as the Lord above breathes life into my body. I cry so much every day because I'm tired of waking up and going to sleep with something deadly inside me, not knowing if I will wake up from that sleep. It really worries me because of the dangerous diseases I have inside me. It's scary, I tell you.

Like I said, today is gone, so live life happily because all the days of our lives are getting shorter, and we don't even realize it. How can people not cry when hurt? I do when I'm hurt, sad, feeling down, and blue. This list of feelings I have inside me is everlasting, for life and then some too. I'm telling you, this list is big and never-ending.

I may not be perfect, and I'm not a robot. But one thing I can say to everyone in this world is that I'm me, an author, a good one, and the last one left of my family too. So I keep hope alive inside of me, along with faith, strength, and God's will, and it doesn't get any better than that if you know what I mean.

I never know what I'm going to say when writing this book here for you and everyone to read. Whatever comes to mind, whatever I feel inside, that comes out when I delve deep into writing. Not a lot of things, but I'm an author of two books, written, made, and done by me. How many of you can say that? Because it sure was hard writing them, I tell you that. It wasn't easy.

I just want the world and everyone in it to know that it was really written, made, and done by me, Rodney Ricks, the last author, the last of me, and the last one that's left at the top of my family. I have a proud mother and father whom I love so much, and I would defend them at any cost, unless, of course, it was God, my Lord above, who was involved.

Ha, you never know what I'm going to say when writing this book of mine. It's a real one, and you won't know until reading it. It's the best one yet, and more are to come. All I want is a legacy, something I did for my family, and for the world, and that's to leave my name behind with two books written and created by me. That's all.

One life, one day, and one I left here on this earth, so it has to be big because this one is the last one left, like me, the last one left of the family. I'm trying very hard to be all I can be in this world as an author of two books made by me. Mom always said, "Who better than you to write a book, books, about feelings?"

The world of diabetes, a never-ending disease, is never going to end until we all pass away, which sucks. But what can you do about that? It's a no-win situation. Dream big, for dreams are going to come true. Better days are coming for you, said the Lord from up above. Just believe in me, and all your dreams will come true.

I love my Father above for all he has done and is still doing for me in life. Live for him today, tomorrow, and every day of your life. You never know what I'm going to say when writing this very last book of mine. It never ends but has to end somewhere. Going and going, I can when it comes to writing in my book, books, written and created by me. But there comes a time where you have to end the story, to make it better for all to read, love, cherish, cry, laugh, enjoy, and more. This is the ending of a wonderful book, written by me, the last author, the last of me, the last one left of my family. The end.

About the Author

Rodney Ricks, a fifty-five-year-old resident of Detroit, Michigan, is a former graduate of Mackenzie High School, class of 1988. He loves to cook and write books for the world to read. His second novel, crafted with considerable time and effort, is meant for readers everywhere. It reflects his world and everything in it, including friends, family, loved ones, and a world filled with people with disabilities.